# Paperwork

# PAPERWORK

Steven Payne

To order additional copies of this book, contact:
Xlibris
800-056-3182
www.Xlibrispublishing.co.uk
Orders@Xlibrispublishing.co.uk
800285

In loving memory

Rhona Sonia Shafik
4 July 1951 – 17 November 2018

Also by Steven Payne and available from Xlibris:

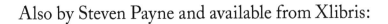

*Carrying the Torch*

*My Lost Prize*

*Love Letters: Great Literary Romances*

*Love Poems*

Her death was the worst thing
that could happen,
and caring for her was best.
— Donald Hall, 'Ardor'

# NOTE

These poems were written over the winter and spring of 2018-19 in the aftermath of the illness and death of the love of my life and partner of twenty-one years, Rhona Shafik, in November 2018.

S.P.

August 2019

# CONTENTS

# COMMENTARY

My wife is dead, who did not care
for or understand poetry, mine the least
of any of it. I didn't, don't mind;
after all there is a world elsewhere
and I made her mine, pieced
together day by succeeding day.
We were loving, furious, tender, unkind
and everything else of which lives are made.
We loved long and happily, goodness knows.
But not ever after. Nobody does anyway.

# Anon

In the windy streets I am no one. In the shops, no one.
No one in the post office, the chemist or the paper shop.
I am unspecial. I do not generally divulge
my status as The Widower with which I've been left,
and dissemble the fact that I am undone.
People who know are kind and hasten to stop
me in the street, knowing by osmosis torment,
fumbling for words, embarrassed by their embarrassment.
Only at home, mostly pissed most nights, do I indulge
the delicious self-pity of the newly bereft.

# Flotsam

One day I'll follow you wherever you went,
my love — but now there is a house to clear
of the flotsam of the couplehood of us
from all our troubled, loving years
as with any couple in any home;
an almost empty bottle of your favourite scent
on the dressing table still where you set it down,
sweet, floral, golden; just as ruinous,
hanging limply on the door all your dressing gowns;
bras and knickers in drawers; shoes beneath the stairs;
toothbrush still in its pot; sundry combs
(I note with tears) not bearing any stray hairs.
All these relics and remnants, all
this wreckage of a curtailed life …
I want to tell everyone I may meet,
I want to call out to unknown people, call
to uncomprehending strangers in the street
and show them these things; I want to say
look; look at this bottle, these socks, this tray —
look; these things were touched once by my wife.

# TACET

The night brings a hard and a glittering frost;
in the morning, brilliant sun;
I demand of both explanation, and yet answer
comes there none.

The moon, waxing toward fullness,
sails free of musket-round cloud; I ask it why
but the moon is as impassive as ever
and gives no reply.

The birds that chatter in my garden
ignore every plea for answers and spurn
all my importunate questioning
and remain taciturn.

# It's the Most Wonderful Time of the Year

I deck the halls with plastic holly,
fa-la-la-la-la; drape the no less fake tree
with lights and baubles, feigning festive
cheer in a house with no festivities.

For an hour or more I pant back and forth
to and from the loft ladder, this year
as every other year with crates of plastic tat,
momentarily paused by scalding tears.

My soul, if there is a soul, I tear asunder, doing all this;
tomorrow night bright lights will dazzle on a tree
heavy with cheap gewgaws in their Christmas place
that last year you saw and now will never see.

# Paperwork

Dodging across Bowling Green Road in between cars,
through glass doors and up thickly-carpeted stairs
to a soft-voiced, professionally sad, defensively-desked registrar
in a bland room of helpful leaflets and insufficient chairs.
Names (maiden and married), times, illnesses, places, dates;
fountain pen proffered: will you please sign here?
Please check all the particulars.
Yes, we take debit cards for certificates—
paperwork invisible through intermittent tears.

Here is what is most painfully true:
I think of not thinking of you
and by that thought think of you all the more.
And there it is again, like a cinder
gone astray and fallen onto tinder.
I am my own fuel of ostensibly infinite store,
self-kindling, fated to burn and yet not yet to die;
condemned to an inferno, doomed
to sear and char like the bush in Sinai
which burned and burned and was not consumed.

# LIGHT

Every morning the candle before your photograph is lit;
day after day, again and again and again,
like yesterday and like tomorrow. I sit
watching it in the miasma of my own pain.

Its orange flame glows in the glass
between when I rise and when I lay
down once more for half-sleep. I pass
it a dozen or more times a day.

There might, I suppose, be some future day
when I finally stop doing this
each day. I shall mourn again and say,
this is the second death; something else to miss.

# BED

By the bed, your almost finished perfume;
umpteen nail varnishes; lotions
for hands; nail files; cotton pads;
nail varnish remover; scissors. The room

would reek of acetone. Anyone would think
it was a nail salon; the clutter,
the impedimenta; all those bottles,
the emery boards, the clippers, that acrid stink.

What do men do with these things
when their wives are dead? Can they be
recycled, or passed on, or do they go
as with so much else into the bin?

I am in the litter of a life and am confused.
All these things of a wife — where do they go
when there are no nails to be painted,
all the stuff of a vanished life lying unused?

# ENGLAND EXPECTS

Men like me must learn to unlearn
the habits of the couple, adopt the role
of the stoical recently-widowed;
must learn to be half, not whole.

Men like me must shop and wash
and cook and clean in a house alone
and are expected to get it wrong,
especially by women with a man of their own.

Men like me are allowed a few tears
when stopped in the street for commiseration
and consolation by kindly folk.
It's all a part of the widower's condition.

Men like me must learn widower's ways;
to learn to make do, to manage, to be all right,
and let everyone gloss over the awkwardness
of the hysterical weeping in the dead of night.

# ROYAL MAIL

The phone is silent but letters still arrive —
junk mail for recycling, genuine mail both —
with your name on, as though you were alive
and awaiting post;

post sent and arriving out of the blue
from faceless companies who still write
knowing where you are and what happened to you
no more than I.

# PERFECT

Now — needless to say — you're perfect,
since we've shed
all the petty annoyances, little gripes
of life; now, instead
of the irritations, minor spats, some stand-up rows,
about your head
clings, glowing, for ever that aureate nimbus
of the perfect dead.

# IGNORANCE

My love, the things I do not know are numerous:
if there are gods, or life beyond death,
and so many other things no human
can be certain of. This I do know:
once upon a time there was a woman
and a man in love who loved her so.
Are you somewhere where you remember us?
I too will one day follow you when I run out of breath
and that is all right. I have been brave alone again today.
My love, my love, I am on my way.

# Night and Day

Days I can beguile with busy-ness
and chores and tasks vital and vain.
Nights, far less.

In the hateful light of day I can move
about my jobs with relative ease.
Darkness I love,

but darkness brings also the lonely
hours that yawn until another daybreak.
If only, if only

you were here with me still today,
my beloved, had that long siege of sickness
not spirited you away.

# Cold Snap

The cold snap is upon us. There may be snow
here, as far north there is already,
bearing the brunt of January weather
according to the news this very minute.
It's one more thing you will not see.
You won't, as before, see it come and go.
You will not leave any trace in it —
footprint or tyre track either —
and, if it comes, will in due
course disappear, as have you.

I do my work about as well as I know.
wish I still smoked; drink; write;
eat barely; vacuum; drink more; try to read;
drink more; write more; walk the dog at night
along the same path where we usually go;
be bored by the television; drink more; feed
the cats and the dog; fill the sink and wash up;
remember that your life has stopped; wish mine would stop.

Snow may be upon us, says the forecast,
sugaring the ground with its icy white
as my photos attest happened last

January. Yes, of course I'll wrap up warm
in the frigid days and bitterer nights.
Full winter outfit. I give you my word
and will try not to try to come to harm.
Outside I'll wear the blue hat that you preferred,
meanwhile trying my hardest not to dwell, as I go,
on just one set of footprints — if it comes — in the snow.

# MUSEUM

Eight weeks the widower, I have lived
in this museum of our life together
so far, surrounded by your things all day.
I would, if I could, linger here for ever,

but know I cannot, and have to leave
this place we made, to live alone
on the proceeds of love and memory
in another home that can never be home.

Most of the exhibits will have to go.
Many binned; some sold; some passed on
to the needy; the ones I cannot bear
to lose I'll have with me, when I'm gone.

# Exile

I am an alien here, and do not like this land.
I do not like its ugly views, its landscapes,
its vistas, its holes and corners.
I am an alien here, and do not like this land.

I did not choose to be here, and I rebel.
I should be at home, not here. This was not
my wish. This is not my place to be.
I did not choose to be here, and I rebel.

I did not ask for any of this.
The manifest injustice of it makes me reel,
the sheer scale of the wrongness of it all.
I did not ask for any of this.

I have made many wrong choices: I did not choose this.
Nobody would choose this: the meaninglessness,
desperation, longing for death, the agony of it all.
I have made many wrong choices: I did not choose this.

# SILENCE

At six o'clock the dark hours are coming.
"Solitude loses its soft power
And loneliness takes over."[1]

Without the telly or your beloved radio
the house is all but silent. Silence
congeals like honey on a cold day,

collecting in corners like evening shadow,
lingering around furniture like untouched dust,
clinging to empty rooms just vacated.

At night I leave the radio on quietly
as you did; for me, not to escape silence
but because you loved its banal chatter.

I was comfortable with silence; you less.
Now, not so much. Only the clock ticking
reminds me of the hours I spend

in busy-ness or drink or nothing very much
of anything at all in particular; only observing
silence settling about me, now you're away.

---

[1]   Donald Hall

# About Time

Unlike me, your tears were rare,
kept like a best outfit for special occasions.
Perhaps not more than a dozen times
in twenty-one years did I see you weep.

The universe balances itself out
in some ways. All your unshed tears
I shed now; on your behalf — yours,
but mostly mine. About time.

# SICK

The litany of the chronically sick:
Renacet; Forceval; Paracetamol;
Allevyn gentle border; Losartan;
Codeine; Fostair; Alfacalcidol.

In hospital, not at home, there were more —
infusions of urokinase,
clot-clouting four-hour injections;
superhero medications such as Alteplase,

and doubtless others I've forgotten.
Most doled out daily from your box of pills
dutifully every morning; a constant
assault upon your sundry ills,

keeping them at bay only so long
until they proved at the last too poor
as remedies to remedy, and to keep
that unwelcome but persistent visitor from our door.

# OBLIVIOUS

The animals are oblivious. Tilly, still
pretty but dim, snores away four-fifths
of her days and nights on the windowsill.

The cats too seem to be ignorant
altogether of the nowhere of you now;
besides affection they merely want

their feed and the occasional dish of cream.
They don't appear, so far as I can tell,
to miss you at all. Lucky them.

They seem to enjoy their little lives,
knowing nothing of pain and grief, remorse,
loneliness, terror of the future. Or vanished wives.

# Death Poet's Society

O may I join that choir all-too-visible
of grief-wracked men who write verses to dead wives;
laments for lost spouses, replete with detail,
replete with memories of dual lives.

Always to hand, Donald Hall's *Without* and *The Painted Bed*;
Douglas Dunn's *Elegies*;
Christopher Reid's *A Scattering*,
Michel Faber's *Undying* and others like these.

I lack their gift but not their loss;
neither their pain nor their desolation,
their constant wound, the fear, the rage;
same lack; same absence; same privation.

# STEPS

Of course you were altered
by abiding sickness. The stairs
up the wooden hill to Bedfordshire
would become for you
little by little your Everest or K2.
I can still see you struggling here,
as the maladies began to consume
all energy. As the ailing heart faltered
piecemeal it would become
harder and harder to do
the thirteen steps to that room,
pausing half-up, panting for precious air.
Thirteen steps. Unlucky for some.
But then, some of us have heart trouble too.

# THE CHRISTMAS CACTUS

The Christmas cactus that you kept trying to kill,
putting it outside in frost until I brought it in,
flourishes to this day on the windowsill.

No gardener, a little cactus in a pot
is about as much as I can tend — and do,
with water every few days in its sunlit spot,

taking snaps when its bright
and cheery flowers appear; soon to fall
but beautiful when they catch the light.

It withstands my ignorance and survives
my clodhopping ministrations.
In fact you might even say it thrives.

You should have known I let no thing
large or small die at my hands; all
things with life should go on living.

Most of my plants fairly quickly die.
The chillies that I tried to grow
were a doomed experiment. But still: I

can't, as I know to my cost,
save everything, and that some
lives will inevitably be lost.

But let life thrive where it may.
I can tend only a cheap plant now;
cheap but lovely in its way.

Life lives until its course is run.
My Christmas cactus (which you tried to kill)
will live another day to see the sun.

# REPORT

Eighty days on, eleven weeks gone,
the house is emptying
but in good shape. The animals are OK. I'm none
of those. Days are bad but busy; nights another thing.

I am heart-sick and have no more taste
for much more life. But our tale was rare.
I can, for a while, live a little longer and waste
no time in its telling. It should be shared.

# Upon All the Living and the Dead

The dead, if poetry and bereavement books
are to be believed,
want the living to let them go. But no;
I will have to grieve

until my own hurtful span is run.
Damn the books. So,
whatever the harm pop psychology says,
I will not let you go.

# THE IMPOSSIBLES

Four months gone I can,
somehow, accommodate;
but the further occasions
I cannot date.

"This time a year back."
"My wife died two years ago."
"Five years ago my wife died."
I do not know

How to deal with such
dates; all of these
remembrances of love,
all these anniversaries.

# TOWNIE

Always urban, nature was never your field —
unlike me, village raised, always on the edge
of an illimitable patchwork of greens.
Nevertheless a few times I coaxed you into
what you thought a strange, mildly anxious wilderness —
no cars, no shops, no people; only
birdsong and sheep and quiet greenery.
Soul balm to me, unrest to you, and
glad to leave quickly. Bless you;
you never knew the peace it brings.

# THE VIGIL

The clock doles out its dull and tawdry hours
between my rising and another attempt at sleep.
In the vacant rooms of the home that was ours
the daily vigil of the widower I keep,

limping from one haggard dawn to another;
hung over often, always sad.
Oh, joy and pride, ally, lover —
such a time, such times, such a life we had.

# SELVES

All these selves — some still living, some long dead —
The Drunk, The Clown, The Would-Be Writer,
The Mentally-Ill Man, The Unwed
Husband, So-Called Poet, The Philanderer,
Chief Cook and Bottlewasher, unpaid
carer, cleaner and nursemaid,
and now the latest: The Widower.
Some are badges of honour; some are open sores.
Now whatever it is I am to be
is a thing to be decided by me:
a job I do not want, since it was rightfully yours.

# Number Not Recognised

Pain awaits me upstairs in your shoes on the floor;
in your toothbrush and all your combs it waits for me;
in the jewellery boxes full of bracelets and rings
and in the nightclothes hanging on the door.
Its worst extremity lurks, it may be,
in the disconnected number I cannot dial any more.
Like it or not lives are made of things,
the paraphernalia which surrounds us all
all our days; some needed, most merely wanted.
It may be that the thing by which I'm most haunted
is the voiceless phone I can no longer call.

# Temps Perdu

Scarcely a thing doesn't transport me:
doesn't evoke some memory,
some remembrance of things past
of the life we led and had so happily.

Sight, sound, taste, scent; a book; the TV;
barely a thing doesn't remind
me of better days than these
cruel days; days that were kind

to us with their gifts of love and harmony
and gentleness and peace. So many hours …
I will have to leave here soon,
but it will, somehow, be always ours.

# SPRING 2019

The daffodils are coming again.
Snowdrops and crocuses too
and branches bursting forth; but then,
all of them are without you.

They are doing it again; the show
of spring, the first after you died,
a spring I never thought to know.
I try to love it but am not mollified

as usual but horrified. The spring show
of blooms in all their loveliness
serves only to remind me of how
much life now is less, so very much less.

How dearly, how deeply you would have adored
this early though transient surprise of spring —
bud and blossom everywhere, more and more;
cloudless afternoon light; the delight of the thing.

The earth turns. Seasons are insistent
and will not, are not to be stayed
by those who have gone, those who went,
or those left to see them anyway.

# Urban Myth

It is not true. It's not true
that the body's cells all renew
each seven years. Certainly their ways
of life and death run at a different pace:

red blood cells some four months; then
white blood cells upwards of a year; the skin
two or three weeks; sperms cells go their way,
like colon cells, after three or four days.

The crucial difference: the cells of the brain
are a one-shot deal and do not come again.
That place in which you are stored —
*in quella parte, dove sta memora* —

keeps its cells life-long. And so,
while the others come and go
in their own sweet time, where you reside
you will reside, as long as I abide

in this world; meaning that memory
of you will stay always with me,
until I join you on this or that day
and follow you, and go your way.

# Autopilot

The days grow shorter for now. Everywhere
are lights. With the dog, houses I pass by
at night are festooned with lights, decorations, trees.
For the last time here I am also doing these

by rote, because we did and would have again.
This time next year, if alive, I will be gone
from our home and will be doing
nothing somewhere else and going

somewhere I shall not, do not wish to be,
where I shall suffer in everything but my longing
to do nothing but to wait to follow my lover
somehow or other, by one means or another.

# THE PERSISTENCE
# OF MEMORY

I can at times half beguile myself to believe
that to walk into the bedroom would be to see
you still luxuriating on the bed, propped up on pillows,
painting your nails to the sound of LBC,

your constant background. Or I might mount the stairs
with lap tray, bringing a mug of tea or food
chosen by you and prepared by me —
fantasies born of sorrow and solitude,

I fully realise. But so real is the dream
that even now to climb the stairs
as I do ten times a day or more and peer
into the bedroom, I might just find you there.

# SNOWDROPS

Snowdrops are lurking in the soil
as a year begins that I do not want.
Will I see them shake their heads again
here, or by then will I be gone?

Leaves will come again to the tree
outside the house, currently bare.
Will I see their slow spring unfolding,
or by then will I be elsewhere?

Spring will come, inevitably.
The Norway maple will bud again
in a few months. Will I note it once more,
or have gone somewhere distant — not home — by then?

Crocuses and daffodils and other spring flowers
will come again in their usual places,
as they are bound to do. I am not sure
if I shall see them, or will have gone without trace.

# SPRING

Daffodils are dancing in the breeze,
crocuses a carpet. The buds that break
from every branch continually amaze.
But you will not wake

for these or anything else like these.
All these signs of spring beyond number
will not now ever trouble your peace
or disturb your slumber;

and whatever springs that I see now,
or may ever see again,
unknowing of the why or the how.
Spring will come; but then

heedless of the both of us. Not spring,
nor its blooms, nor rampant trees,
nor building birds, nor anything.
None of these

will rouse you ever. Not even morning sun
can stir you from whichever place,
call it what you may, wherever you have gone,
leaving such traces.

# WEATHER REPORT

After a grey start (there was rain overnight)
the late afternoon sun is strong and clear, bright
in the eyes of the houses on the opposite
side of our street. On our couch I half-lie, half-sit

thinking of course of the only thing
to be thought of now. It brings
some comfort and much pain and vice versa. I
see the chattering classes fly

past the windows of a home soon not
to be home after eighteen years. What
I am to do, where to go, I'm afraid
I'm at a loss to say. But choices must be made.

Midwinter is seven weeks gone; days are lengthening,
night held at bay daily, daylight strengthening.
Over our little garden the early evening sky is clear,
turning red. Soon, my love, I will not be here.

e dicerò di lei piangendo, pui
che si n'è gita in ciel subitamente,
e ha lasciato Amor meco dolente.
—Dante Alighieri, *La Vita Nuova*, XXXI